D0328920

Inspiring Words

FROM THE
PSALMS

FOR COUPLES

Presented to

Presented by

Date

Inspiring Words FROM THE PSALMS

FOR COUPLES

SPIRIT PRESS

Inspiring Words from the Psalms for Couples
ISBN 1-40372-043-6

Published in 2005 by Spirit Press, an imprint of Dalmatian Press, LLC.
Copyright © 2005 Dalmatian Press, LLC. Franklin, Tennessee 37067.

Scripture quotations marked CEV are from *The Contemporary English Version*.
Copyright © 1991, 1992, 1995 by American Bible Society. Used by permission.

Scripture quotations marked GNT are from the *Good News Translation, Second Edition*,
Copyright © 1992 by American Bible Society. Used by permission. All rights reserved.

Scripture quotations marked THE MESSAGE are taken from *The Message*. Copyright © by
Eugene H. Peterson, 1993, 1994, 1995. Used by permission of NavPress Publishing Group.

Scripture quotations marked NASB are taken from the *New American Standard Bible*.
Copyright © The Lockman Foundation 1960, 1962, 1963, 1968, 1971, 1972, 1973, 1975,
1977, 1995. Used by permission.

Scripture quotations marked NIV are taken from the *Holy Bible, New International
Version*®. NIV ®. Copyright © 1973, 1978, 1984 by International Bible Society. Used by
permission of Zondervan Publishing House. All rights reserved.

Scripture quotations marked NKJV are taken from *The New King James Version*.
Copyright © 1979, 1980, 1982, Thomas Nelson, Inc.

Scripture quotations marked NLT are taken from the *Holy Bible, New Living Translation*,
copyright © 1996. Used by permission of Tyndale House Publishers, Inc., Wheaton, Illinois
60189. All rights reserved.

Scripture quotations marked NRSV are from *The New Revised Standard Version of the Bible*,
Copyright © 1989, 1997 by The Division of Christian Education of the National Council of
the Churches of Christ in the USA. Used by permission. All rights reserved.

Editor: Lila Empson
Writer: Phillip H. Barnhart
Text Designer: Whisner Design Group

Printed in China. All rights reserved under International Copyright Law. Contents and/or
cover may not be reproduced in whole or in part in any form without the express written
consent of the Publisher.

05 06 07 WAI 10 9 8 7 6 5 4 3 2 1

You will show me the path that leads to life;
your presence fills me with joy
and brings me pleasure forever.

PSALM 16:11 GNT

Contents

Introduction

Marriage is the sweetest fellowship this side of heaven. It puts love in your heart, light on your path, and gives life to all you do. It brings to you the joy of angels. Marriage paints your life in bright and vivid colors and sings to you a melody of rare and exquisite beauty. It gives you encouragement for each day, and reason to celebrate at the end of each day. Marriage makes everything better.

Your marriage gives you reason to count and recount your blessings. As you read this book and walk heart and heart through its pages, you will feel warmth and excitement in the presence of each other. You will reflect, share, and know how good it is to be together. You will see God's fingerprints all over your marriage. You will drink out of your saucer because your cup has overflowed.

*Y*ou know me inside and out, you hold me together,
you never fail to stand me tall in your presence
so I can look you in the eye.

PSALM 41:12 THE MESSAGE

Your Love Is Good

I will exult and rejoice in your steadfast love.

PSALM 31:7 NRSV

Your love for each other is good. It brings to your lives fresh joy and new purpose. It gives you a destiny to walk toward together and reason to celebrate each step of the way. Your love enlightens what you think, invigorates what you feel, and enables what you do. It inaugurates the day and commends the night. It gives focus, provides encouragement, and makes all things meaningful.

Because you love each other, your hearts are always young. Love is at the center of your world. It makes your world go around. It makes the ride worthwhile. Your love makes you smile when you are tired and persevere when you are challenged. You rejoice in all things. You share your love with each other, and it multiplies. Your love is a doorway through which you enter room after room of possibility and power.

Your love is a blessing. It brings warmth to your hearts and lights up your world. Your love is wonderful.

May your constant love
be with us, LORD, as we
put our hope in you.

PSALM 33:22 GNT

Gifts to Each Other

Praise the LORD, O my soul,
and forget not all his benefits.

PSALM 103:2 NIV

You are God's gifts to each other. Just as Eve came to Adam from God, you came to one another from the bounty of heaven. Your marriage opened the storehouse of God's goodness and poured out on you the blessing of one another. Because of each other, you have love, life, and laughter. You have purpose, possibility, and power. Through the one to whom you are married, you drink from the cup of divine giftedness. You sit at the fire of God's plan and purpose for you.

Good things happen in your marriage because you know God blessed you with each other. Because you see your marriage through sacred eyes, gratitude increases. You are thoughtful and kind. You take good care of each other. You are optimistic and forward thinking. You are creative in thought and courageous in action. You step higher and walk farther.

God gave you to each other. You are
blessings from God for one another.

The LORD will bless
them and save them;
God will declare them
innocent.

PSALM 24:5 GNT

Serving God Together

Serve the LORD with gladness; come
before Him with joyful singing.

PSALM 100:2 NASB

*M*ary and Joseph perceived marriage as a place to serve God. Their home would house God's Son, their love would nourish a Messiah, their teaching would establish a foundation on which Jesus would build his career for God.

In your marriage, you can serve God. You can have a vocation of faith and works on behalf of God, who gives you to each other. You can fulfill God's purpose in your marriage.

At a retreat for married couples, the leader asked why those present had come. One man's answer was special. "I have come for three reasons," he said. "I love God, and I have come to get closer to God. I love my wife, and I have come to get closer to her. And both my wife and I have come to learn how we can better serve God together."

You belong to God and to each other. You can
serve God together. You can make God's love real
wherever you are.

Lord our God, may
your blessings be with
us. Give us success in
all we do!

Psalm 90:17 GNT

Marriage on Fire

He spread out a cloud as a covering,
and a fire to give light at night.

PSALM 105:39 NIV

Chad, seven years old, attended a wedding with his neighbors in their church. He watched every part of the service with interest and

was especially curious about why one of the three candles on the altar was not lighted, the one in the middle. Chad heard the minister say something about the candles on the altar and saw the bride and groom go there and stand in front of them. The bride lifted the candle on the left, the groom lifted the candle on the right, and together they lighted the candle in the middle. The minister talked about the bride and groom becoming like one person.

When Chad got home, his mother asked him what kind of wedding it was. Chad thought and thought about his mother's question. Then he said, "The pastor said it was the kind where 'two people get ignited.'"

Your marriage was made to bring a warmth
that no cold can overcome and a light
that no darkness can put out.

Light, space, zest—
that's GOD! So, with
him on my side I'm
fearless, afraid of no
one and nothing.

PSALM 27:1 THE MESSAGE

Think Big

He has set a tabernacle for the sun, which is like a bridegroom coming out of his chamber, and rejoices like a strong man to run its race.

PSALM 19:4–5 NKJV

Think big about your marriage. It brightens each day with its charm and communion. It makes the night a restful and peaceful place. Your marriage shares the burdens of daily life and increases the joy of your experiences. It clears paths through difficulties, builds bridges over brokenness, and scales mountains of unexpected challenges. Your marriage is founded on trust, respect, and love. It is competent and capable.

Your marriage sings a song of hope in the midst of everyday problems, rings a bell of courage when life throws a curve, and writes a sonnet of optimism by whose rhythm and rhyme you march boldly and confidently. Your marriage makes each minute an unrepeatable miracle, brings to small happenings a spectacular delight, and gives you a beautiful life each day. Your marriage is strong, deep, and good.

Think big about your marriage. Be honest about what is. Your marriage is the greatest!

Wait for the Lord; be strong and take heart and wait for the Lord.

Psalm 27:14 niv

Over and Over

Good people will prosper like palm trees,
grow tall like Lebanon cedars.

PSALM 92:12 THE MESSAGE

A successful marriage means falling in love many times with the same person. It doesn't work when you put your marriage on automatic pilot. It won't fly for long on its initial propulsion. A successful marriage requires many fuel injections along the way, and four hands on the wheel at all times. *Go Right On Working* to *grow* a marriage.

Marriage is like an extension ladder. Every time you get to the top, throw up another extension and keep climbing. God honors those who expand their horizons and find new cadences by which to march. Continue courtship, repeat romance, and be redundant with both the experience and the expression of love. Think beyond being married, as if it happens only one time. Plan to be always marrying. The wedding is a one-time event, but the marriage is an ongoing process, always open to new possibilities and new power.

Marriage is an ever-increasing opportunity to know
the highest quality of human relationship.

You send abundant rain
on the plowed fields and
soak them with water;
you soften the soil with
showers and cause the
young plants to grow.

Psalm 65:10 GNT

The Right Ones

O LORD, you have searched me and you know me.

PSALM 139:1 NIV

You are the right people for your marriage. Answers you need are in your hearts, ideas that move marriage forward are in your heads,

insights to solve problems belong to you. Strength for the road and perseverance for the climb are found in the core of your faith. You are like Moses when God pointed to the resource that was in his hand, or Peter, who had what it took to start a church, or David, whose seemingly small rocks were enough to bring down a giant and save a people.

Look within because you have what it takes. Turn to yourselves because you are what is needed. Seek what is to be found inside you. Ask questions, knowing you have the answers to them. Knock on your own doors, and they will open.

Respond to the ability within yourselves. Drink from the depths of your own wells. Move out in the strength of your own strides.

I take joy in doing
your will, my God,
for your will is written
on my heart.

PSALM 40:8 NLT

Addition That Multiplies

I'm thanking you, GOD, from a full heart,
I'm writing the book on your wonders.

PSALM 9:1 THE MESSAGE

Marriage is greater than the groom. Marriage is greater than the bride. It is greater than the groom and the bride together. The sum of the parts of marriage is more than the parts themselves. Marriage is addition that multiplies.

What makes marriage larger than the bride and groom is God's presence in the marriage. When you invite God to your marriage he comes, and when he comes, his love for you and his commitment to your marriage make it larger. His love for you inspires your love for each other. His commitment to your marriage sends you deeper into your devotion to one another. In marriage, you are enhanced by God's concern for you, enlarged by God's care of you, and expanded by God's walk with you.

Commitment to marriage makes everything larger.
Potential increases, provision enlarges, ability
expands. You are more than before.

You are faithful, and I
trust you because you
rescued me.

PSALM 31:5 CEV

Invitation List

He won't let you stumble,
your Guardian God won't fall asleep.

PSALM 121:3 THE MESSAGE

All over the country black-and-white billboards popped up containing various messages from God. One message said, "Loved the wedding. Invite me to the marriage."

When you invite God to your marriage, he comes. He comes to help you do more with your marriage than you can do with it by yourselves. By yourselves, you have only human abilities to call on. When you are partners with God in your marriage, there is a greater deposit from which you can withdraw assistance. Resources abound. Intermittent springs from which to drink are everywhere. God's *presence* keeps you company on a daily basis. God's *purpose* gives you meaningful work to do together. God's *power* sends you forth into life as a courageous and confident couple. And God is in it all.

Invite God into your lives, and he will walk up and down the aisle of your marriage each and every day.

Inspiring Words FROM THE PSALMS

My help will come from the LORD, who made heaven and earth.

PSALM 121:2 GNT

Redundantly Romantic

I, through the abundance of your steadfast love,
will enter your house.

PSALM 5:7 NRSV

On a downtown city street, a young man knelt on the sidewalk and proposed marriage to his sweetheart. Cameras flashed, people applauded, and joy sang its way through the air. Hearty handshakes and exuberant hugs of congratulation went all around. The young man had arranged everything beforehand. He invited friends, hired a photographer, and had a caterer standing by at a local restaurant. At the restaurant, an older man walked over to the groom-to-be, put his hand on his shoulder and said, "Nice going, young man, now keep it up."

Be a romantic. Love your mate enough to be creative in thought and forthright in action. Put your mind in a search mode, pursuing fresh ways to express your love. Move forward from thought to action with cards, notes, flowers, timely remembrances, and special events. Miss no opportunity to say "I love you."

Romance is the language of love. Speak it clearly
and speak it often. The language of love is heard.

I love you, LORD
God, and you
make me strong.

PSALM 18:1 CEV

Love Discovers

I will remember my song in the night;
I will meditate with my heart, and my spirit ponders.

PSALM 77:6 NASB

Love is discovery without end. As long as you search for significance and meaning in your marriage, your love lives and flourishes. What you look for, you find, and in the finding, you are elevated beyond expectation and illuminated beyond prediction. Marriage is a quest for abundant living that brings with it unequaled joy and gladness. When you seek quality and excellence in your marriage, you discover hidden joys of life.

Archimedes, a Greek mathematician, stepped into his bath one day and made a fantastic discovery. As he watched the displaced water spill out of the bath, he understood how metals could be weighed. He ran out of his house and raced down the street shouting, "I have found it! I have found it!" There is no excitement like that of discovery.

Love searches until it finds. When it finds, there is
great joy and celebration. All are jubilant.

Search me, O God, and know my heart.

PSALM 139:23 NIV

Free to Love

How exquisite your love, O God!

PSALM 36:7 THE MESSAGE

You love your mate. God not only gives you the ability to love, but he also gives you permission to love. Love is what God wants you to do. It is God's deep desire that you experience love for the one you marry and that you express what you experience in uncontestable ways. God wants you to know love, and God wants you to show beyond doubt what you know. Feel it, reveal it, don't conceal it. Express it, don't repress it. Let go and let love rush forth as a flowing stream.

To love is to leave yourself and go to the other. It is to be free to take risks, innovate ideas, look for fresh horizons, and imagine great happenings. It is to be excessive, exuberant, and extravagant. Love gives you wings with which to fly.

Love with all the stops out. Turn all the pages. Tear down all the fences. Let love loose.

*H*e answered me
and set me free.

PSALM 118:5 GNT

Come On In

I trust in God's unfailing love for ever and ever.

PSALM 52:8 NIV

*I*nvite each other into all the rooms of your lives. Don't leave your marriage mate sitting out on the porch. Open the door wide and give

an all-out welcome. Grab your mate by the heart and give a tour of everything you are—upstairs where your dreams reside and downstairs where your secrets hide, in the front and out back. Explore all you have been, are now, wish you were, and want to be. Relate experiences, pleasant and otherwise. Reveal tendencies, inclinations, habits. Acknowledge mistakes, give voice to hopes, talk about all of it.

Take your arms from around your life and say, "Come on in!" Don't play hide-and-seek. Put out a welcome mat to your heart. Make your invitation all-inclusive, without disclaimer or qualification. Be accessible and reachable. Withhold nothing. Share everything.

Be open and vulnerable. Share your heart. Make yourself known. Be someone who can be loved.

*Y*our love and loyalty
will always keep me safe.

PSALM 40:11 GNT

Even After

Blessed be the LORD, the God of Israel,
from everlasting to everlasting.

PSALM 41:13 NRSV

*T*he secret to a good marriage is learning how to live happily *even after*. Even after surprises that sneak up on you and throw you a curve. Even after unexpected sickness, bad job experiences, broken promises. Even after colic and dirty diapers.

Better than the prince who comes and takes you away on a white steed or the princess who glitters with glamour at the ball is the person who stays with you in all circumstances and sticks with you no matter what, someone who stays in the boat with you even when it leaks. Loyalty and love make a marriage successful. Loyalty doesn't always agree with what you say but listens while you say it. Even if love has gone missing, loyalty bridges the gap until love returns.

Your marriage grows when you both keep on
keeping on. Hanging in there together makes
marriage strong and deep.

If I ascend into heaven,
You are there; if I make
my bed in hell, behold,
You are there.

PSALM 139:8 NKJV

What It Looks Like

Shout praises to the LORD! He is good to us,
and his love never fails.

PSALM 107:1 CEV

A teacher had her third graders draw pictures of what they wanted to be when they grew up. They drew firefighters, doctors, actresses, basketball players, astronauts, and people in other predictable occupations. There were no surprises until one little girl turned in a blank sheet of paper. The teacher didn't know what to think about that because Jodi usually did the best of anybody. "Jodi," said the teacher, "why didn't you draw something? Don't you know what you want to be when you grow up?"

"Oh yes, Mrs. Jenkins," she replied, "I want to be married, but I don't know how to draw it."

You draw your marriage with a passion that finds expression, a love that knows faithfulness, and a commitment that won't let go. You draw it with God's hand on yours.

Your marriage is a picture you draw together with your mate. Choose your colors carefully and paint boldly.

I say to GOD, "Be my Lord!"
Without you, nothing makes sense.

PSALM 16:2 THE MESSAGE

Continue Commitment

Commit your way to the LORD,
trust also in Him, and He will do it.

PSALM 37:5 NASB

Don't let your marriage commitment get any older than twenty-four hours. Renew your pledge to each other on a daily basis. It is continuing commitment to marriage that gives it strength, purpose, and destiny. It is your everyday pledge to loyalty, trust, and dedication that puts wheels under your marriage and makes it go.

Be steadfast whether the situation is richer or poorer, better or worse, sickness or health. Commitment accepts changes and variables. It adjusts to surprises, adapts to turns in the road. Let your mate know you are sticking alongside no matter what. Commitment to continuity paves roads and builds bridges. Commitment to going all the way creates a rich and deep marriage. Commitment meets no challenge that it can't overcome. Commitment is better than anything else you can give your marriage.

Do what you ought to do when you ought
to do it for as long as it takes.

I will praise the LORD
while I live; I will sing
praises to my God while
I have my being.

PSALM 146:2 NASB

Keep Up the Interest

You notice everything I do and everywhere I go.

PSALM 139:3 CEV

Be interested in your mate. Be attentive to your marriage. Keep your marriage on the front burner of priority. Be more interested in your marriage than in your job, hobby, or your children. Show your interest in tangible ways. Reach out and hold his hand. Put your arm around her shoulder. Prop a note of affirmation against the morning cup of coffee.

Select something about your mate that makes you proud, and make sure your mate knows what it is. Marriage is a duet in which when one sings the other claps. Remember all special days. Treat ordinary days in special ways. Make long-range plans. Create surprises. Every now and then, go over the top. Check regularly with your mate about how he is feeling, what she would like to do during the weekend. When needed, read between the lines. Show you care by being aware.

The bonds of matrimony are a good investment when the interest is kept up.

My frame was not
hidden from you,
when I was being
made in secret.

PSALM 139:15 NRSV

Hold Hands

You hold me by my right hand.

PSALM 73:23 NKJV

Harry and Bess Truman had one of the great romances of history. No matter the circumstances, their focus was on each other. When Truman, as president of the United States, was negotiating with Churchill and Stalin across the world on a ship, he would leave in the middle of a conference and have naval personnel contact Bess on shortwave radio so he could talk to her. Bess often went over the heads of those protecting the president to get in touch with him. The two of them were sometimes seen strolling out behind the White House, out of sight of Secret Service agents.

One time a reporter asked Bess about their relationship, and she said, "Harry and I have been sweethearts and married more than forty years, and no matter where I was, when I put out my hand Harry's was there to grasp it."

Touching is a most eloquent way to show affection. Touching is always understood.

Hold me,
and I will be safe.

PSALM 119:117 GNT

Good Treatment

Look down from heaven and see,
and take care of this vine.

PSALM 80:14 NASB

*I*n the musical *My Fair Lady*, Eliza Doolittle, comparing Henry Higgins with Colonel Pickering, says, "The difference between a lady

and a flower girl is not how she behaves but how she is treated."

Kindness shown all around brings out the best in your marriage. When you are kind, you are not blind to needs and necessities. Your kindness seeks out empty places and fills them with concern and consideration. It recognizes wounds for what they are and anoints them with gentle tenderness. It knows when your mate has fallen and quickly offers a lifting hand. Kindness sees what might occur and prevents it from happening. Kindness offers patience and grants acceptance. Even the smallest act of kindness reverberates across your marriage, enriching and deepening it. Remember, at all times in your marriage, it is more important to be kind than to be right.

Kindness comes in a straight line. It is a language each
of you can speak and each of you can understand.

The LORD is just in all his ways, and kind in all his doings.

PSALM 145:17 NRSV

Know Who You Have

All Your works shall praise You, O LORD,
and Your saints shall bless You.

PSALM 145:10 NKJV

Baseball great Tommy Lasorda frequently speaks in public about his marriage. He seldom misses an opportunity to speak highly of the relationship he has with his wife. Often in an interview he changes the subject so he can tell a love story from personal experience. He has a marriage he likes to talk about. Asked one time to give some of his thoughts about marriage, he began by saying, "I have a great wife. If I could have seen God one week before I got married and had written down on a piece of paper what I wanted for a wife, he couldn't have given me a better one than I have."

Appreciate who you have in your marriage. Say "thank you" and "well done" frequently. Be generous with tokens of appreciation. Be vocally grateful. Love your mate out loud.

The best word you can say to your mate is "thanks." Seize every opportunity to say it.

Let me tell his greatness
in a prayer of thanks.

PSALM 69:30 THE MESSAGE

Stronger Together

O magnify the LORD with me, and let us exalt His name together.

PSALM 34:3 NASB

At a county fair, there was a horse-pulling contest. The first-place horse moved a sled weighing 4,500 pounds. The second-place horse

pulled 4,000 pounds. The owners of the two horses decided to see what they could pull together. They hitched them up, and together they moved 12,000 pounds. Working as a team, they were good for 3,500 more pounds than when each made a separate effort.

Unity in your marriage produces greater results than individual effort. Teamwork divides the effort and multiplies the result. Mutuality brings power to overcome, strength to persevere. Talents are pooled and abilities blended. Skills complement each other in a kaleidoscopic array of quality and efficiency. Strength comes from one of you to the other, and both of you are strong. Shared insight measures your problems and then cuts them down to size. You and your mate do better in harness.

The key concept is the "we" concept. Keep together what God put together. Move forward to the beat of one heart.

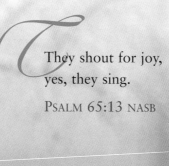 They shout for joy,
yes, they sing.

PSALM 65:13 NASB

The Only One

God, the one and only—I'll wait as long as he says.
Everything I need comes from him.

PSALM 62:1 THE MESSAGE

*I*n the movie *Runaway Bride,* Ike Graham is a journalist who comes to town to do a story on Maggie Carpenter, who has left three men at the altar. Maggie and Ike eventually fall in love, and at their wedding Maggie runs again. Humiliated, Ike goes home, but Maggie follows him and they are subsequently married in a private ceremony.

Before the wedding takes place, Maggie gets on her knees and repeats to Ike the exact words he had previously spoken to her. She says, "I guarantee there will be tough times. I guarantee that at some point one or both of us will want to get out of this thing. But I also guarantee that if I don't ask you to be mine, I'll regret it the rest of my life, because I know in my heart you are the only one for me."

No greater joy exists than when you are the only one for your mate and your mate is the only one for you.

You make my life
pleasant, and my
future is bright.

PSALM 16:6 CEV

Jesus in Attendance

Your goodness is so great! You have stored up
great blessings for those who honor you.

PSALM 31:19 NLT

A little boy in Sunday school class heard the story of the wedding feast in Cana of Galilee, and how Jesus turned water into wine. He was fascinated by what happened there that day. When his dad learned what the story had been, he asked the boy what he had learned from it. The boy thought a couple of minutes and then replied, "If you are going to have a wedding, make sure Jesus is there."

Jesus can change your water into wine. He can take what you give him and make it more than it was. He can help you discover your potential and realize it. Jesus can take the embers of your marriage and fan them into flames. He can nurture the seed you plant, increase the offerings you bring, and bring his power to your marriage when you commit it to him.

Nothing God touches stays the same. Increase is God's
business. All things become more in God's hands.

The earth has yielded its increase; God, our God, has blessed us.

PSALM 67:6 NRSV

One and Only

*You created every part of me; you put me
together in my mother's womb.*

PSALM 139:13 GNT

*J*osh and Evie finished dinner and pulled back from the table.
Dinner had been eaten against the background of a lively and joyful
conversation. Evie had been particularly witty
that evening and had made Josh laugh several
times. Reflecting in the midst of his joy and
thinking about how special his wife was, he
reached his hand toward hers and spoke.
"Evie, do you know what I like best about
you?" Evie blushed and shook her head. Josh
said, "You don't remind me of anyone."

To know and celebrate your mate's unique
characteristics gives you pride. It makes you
grateful you are the one your partner chose. It brings a sense of
excitement, joy, and privilege. Your mate is magnificently different
and excitingly unique. So are you. You are both blessed by the differ-
ences you each bring to your marriage.

*One who is different brings untold blessings. It is
wonderful to be married to one of a kind.*

*Y*ou anoint my head with oil; my cup overflows.

PSALM 23:5 NRSV

Face It Together

Let ocean breakers call out, "Encore!"
And mountains harmonize the finale.

PSALM 98:8 THE MESSAGE

or two weeks before their wedding, Lucretia sent Kenyatta a card each day. She had deliberately chosen the cards for their various messages of affirmation and encouragement. She wanted to create an atmosphere of hope and confidence. She believed that together they were competent and effective, and she wanted to establish that in both their hearts. On the eve of the wedding, Kenyatta went to the mailbox to get Lucretia's card for that day. He opened it and smiled widely as he read the message inside the card: "Baby, forget about the rest—we're the best!"

Marriage consists of more than facing each other and embracing in love and affection. It also consists of holding hands, looking outward in the same direction, and facing courageously and confidently whatever challenges come to your doorstep.

Alone you can do it, but you can't do it alone. Together
you are strong enough to seize and win the day.

My times are in Your
hand; deliver me from
the hand of my enemies
and from those who
persecute me.

PSALM 31:15 NASB

Always Marrying

Oh, continue Your lovingkindness to those who know You.

PSALM 36:10 NKJV

After he was assigned to a mission church in a small town in Peru, a young priest presided at his first wedding there. The priest, having just completed a short course in Spanish and not being nearly as fluent in that language as he'd like to be, concluded the wedding ceremony with these words: "Go now in love and peace. This marriage is finished."

Your marriage is never finished. No one in the history of the world has ever been married, because *married* is past tense. You don't wake up one morning and say, "Now, at this point in my history, I am married." Marriage is never complete, never done. It is always on the move. Marriage is an ongoing and continuing process. When God made marriage, it came out of the long-range planning department.

Think ahead, go forward, climb higher, get better. Always be marrying.

I shall walk before the
LORD in the land of the
living.

PSALM 116:9 NASB

Be Aware

Show me your paths and teach me to
follow; guide me by your truth and instruct me.

PSALM 25:4–5 CEV

While attending a weekend marriage seminar, Todd and Belinda listened as the leader taught a session on communication. He said that

to communicate well in a marriage it was important that wives and husbands know the things that are important to each other. He said to the men, "For instance, gentlemen, can you name your wife's favorite flower?" Todd leaned over, touched Belinda's arm gently, and whispered, "Honey, yours is Pillsbury All Purpose, isn't it?" The rest of the story is not pleasant.

Keep your antenna up in your marriage. Be aware of what's going on with your mate. Know likes and dislikes, preferences and priorities, dreams and desires. Anticipate what your mate wants to do and where your mate wants to go. Be aware of when your mate wants to do nothing and go nowhere. Know your mate like a book.

Sit up and take notice of what makes
your mate sit up and take notice.

Those who know your name trust in you, for you, O LORD, have never abandoned anyone who searches for you.

PSALM 9:10 NLT

Mean Business

I will extol you, my God and King,
and bless your name forever and ever.

PSALM 145:1 NRSV

A mother sat relaxing in the den one evening while her daughter was reading a book about the meaning of names.

"Mother," the daughter said, "Philip means 'lover of horses,' and James means 'beloved.' I wonder what George means?"

At that point, the mother quit relaxing and said to her daughter, "Well, as much as the two of you have been seeing each other, I hope George means business."

Mean business in your marriage. If you are going to be obsessed about something, be obsessed about the health and welfare of your marriage. If you are going to have a compulsion about anything, be compelled to make your marriage a great one. *Have* to have a good marriage, not just *want* to have one. Commit to an unrelenting pursuit of that goal. Make your marriage number one on your "must" list.

Find a way. Make a way.
If the door is closed, break it down.

O pen to me the gates of
righteousness; I shall enter
through them, I shall give
thanks to the LORD.

PSALM 118:19 NASB

Front-Burner Marriage

With God on our side we will win.

PSALM 108:13 GNT

Keep your marriage on the front burner of priority and it will have the heat of passion and the warmth of love. When what ought to be

first is put there, rewards of enlightenment and joy come to your marriage. Move secondary concerns to the back burner, push unimportant items and issues off the stove, and focus on being the couple God had in mind when he made your marriage a matter of divine summons.

Look over your schedule and ask what you would change if you lived it according to what God wants your marriage to be. When a famous sculptor was asked how he made such a beautiful horse, he said he took a block of marble and cut out everything that didn't look like a horse. In your marriage, cut out everything that does not serve God's purpose for your marriage. Put first things where they belong.

Learn to say no to the good in your marriage so you can say yes to the best. Priorities determine your progress in your marriage.

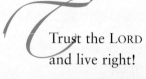

Trust the LORD
and live right!

PSALM 37:3 CEV

Important or Just Urgent

He guides me in paths of righteousness for his name's sake.

PSALM 23:3 NIV

Many things in your marriage are more urgent than they are important. They are the squeaky wheels that call out for your attention but could probably do without it. Sometimes it seems someone has reversed the order, taken high prices and put them on cheap things and put low prices on what really matters. Learn the difference between superficial fluff and authentic stuff in your marriage. Don't let a nickel hold up a dollar, or spend five dollars' worth of time on a fifty-cent issue.

Not everything that's urgent is important. Not everything that's important is urgent. Listen for the sound, often a quiet one, of what is important. Stay focused on the center. Stay away from the circumference. Keep peripheral issues out on the edge where they belong. Live at the heart of your marriage.

Choose the important over the urgent, the ultimate over the immediate. Throw away the oyster and keep the pearl.

The earth is the LORD's,
and everything in it.

PSALM 24:1 NIV

For God's Glory

Lift up your heads, O you gates! And be lifted up, you everlasting doors! And the King of glory shall come in.

PSALM 24:7 NKJV

One evening, Saint Francis sat in the light of the setting sun playing chess with a little boy. A colleague came by and was aghast at

what Francis was doing. "For shame, Brother Francis, that you should play a foolish game with a foolish child. If the Lord suddenly appeared, what would you do?"

Francis didn't have to think about that long, so his reply came shortly. "What would I do? Brother, it is a foolish question. I would finish the game for the glory of God. It was for the glory of God I began it."

In your marriage, begin and finish all things for the glory of God. Do everything to honor and reverence God in your lives. Hold everything as sacred. Make all your marriage a sanctuary for the presence of God.

Make the chief aim of your marriage that of glorifying God. In all you think, say, and do, give God the glory.

O LORD, I love the house in which you dwell, and the place where your glory abides.

PSALM 26:8 NRSV

Battleships or Lighthouses

LORD, lift up the light of Your countenance upon us.

PSALM 4:6 NKJV

One night an admiral on a battleship ordered a certain course, but the navigation officer, seeing a light in the distance, reported that the battleship seemed to be on a collision course with another ship. The

admiral immediately ordered his radio operator to send a message to the oncoming ship demanding that it change its course. The simple reply came quickly: "No, you change your course."

After two more unsuccessful communiqués, the admiral stormed into the radio room, grabbed the microphone, and bellowed into it, "Change your course. I am a battleship!"

After a brief silence, the reply came: "Change your course. I am a lighthouse."

Put your marital battleships in dry dock and head toward lighthouses of harmony and unity. Unclench your fists and open your hands in compromise and forgiveness. Be lovers, not fighters.

Love heals hurt, mends brokenness, and closes wounds. Love reduces friction to a fraction.

You, O LORD, keep my lamp burning;
my God turns my darkness into light.

PSALM 18:28 NIV

It All Depends

I can't wait to hear what he'll say.

PSALM 85:8 THE MESSAGE

A man and a woman walked down a busy street in a big city. Suddenly the woman stopped and said, "I hear a bird chirping."

The man said, rather incredulously, "I don't hear it." He continued, "Anyway, how could you hear a bird chirping here in this chaos and confusion?"

The woman insisted she could hear the bird. "There, I heard it again," she said. The man continued to deny that possibility. Then the woman took a coin out of her purse and, without the man seeing her do it, dropped the coin on the sidewalk. The man immediately looked down and began searching for the coin. The woman laughed and said, "See, it all depends on what you listen for."

Listen for love, light, and life in your marriage. Listen for joy, peace, and comfort. Listen for purpose. Listen for God.

Tune in to what is good and wholesome in your marriage. Listen for sounds of hope and destiny. You hear what you listen for.

*I*f you would
but listen to me.

PSALM 81:8 NIV

Are We There Yet?

You keep me safe, and I always trust you.

PSALM 25:5 CEV

Weddings are special and beautiful but still short of magical. No celestial dust filters down from the canopy of providence to amalgamate two people into one. No one waves a wand over the couple so they can go off in wedding splendor to enter the marriage hall of fame.

Probably at some point in your marriage you'll want to know if you are there yet. Are you where you thought you'd be by now? Sometimes, you climb a long time without even getting near the top. You run far without reaching anything. Is someone moving the goalposts? Saint Augustine said patience is the companion of wisdom, and he was right. It is wise to learn how to wait on those good things you want right now in your marriage. Patience makes heaviness light, chases darkness away, and grows you inwardly in courage and faith.

Patience suspends obstacles. It creates capacity to endure for a purpose. It enables you to sit long enough.

Wait patiently for the LORD. Be brave and courageous. Yes, wait patiently for the LORD.

PSALM 27:14 NLT

Rough Makes Smooth

The LORD is a shelter for the oppressed,
a refuge in times of trouble.

PSALM 9:9 NLT

*J*oan, going through a rough time in her marriage, was watching an animated movie with her husband, Wyatt. The movie was *Mulan*,

a story of a young woman who overcame fierce opposition to reach the goal and seize the prize. Assessing what Mulan was able to accomplish despite substantial obstacles, the emperor says, "The flower that blooms in adversity is the most beautiful flower of all." Hearing that sentiment, Joan reached over to Wyatt, put her hand on top of his, and said, "You and I can be like that flower, can't we?"

Adversity is a good teacher. It trains the mind, fortifies the heart, and challenges the will. When you wrestle honestly with problems in your marriage, your nerves are strengthened and your skill is sharpened. Adversity introduces you to yourself, to the real you who is strong, resolved, and determined.

You are like a tea bag. It is when you are in hot
water that you know how strong you are.

GOD answer you on the
day you crash.

PSALM 20:1 THE MESSAGE

A Wake-Up Call

As for me, I shall behold Your face in righteousness;
I will be satisfied with Your likeness when I awake.

PSALM 17:15 NASB

Stress in a marriage wakes you up to good things you weren't paying attention to. It breaks you away from dependence on the

obvious. It pulls you away from the predictable and gets your creative juices going. When the constancy and regularity you have come to depend on are not there in your marriage, you become more imaginative. When what is supposed to happen doesn't happen, you look for new answers. You create fresh solutions. You go to places in your mind and heart you've not been before.

When something unexpected creates tension and stress in your marriage, you find a new well from which to draw and a new fountain from which to drink. You look for resources not previously known and itemized. You discover hidden abilities and undisclosed strengths. You uncover qualities of character and competence of endeavor you'd forgotten about, or didn't know existed. Your cream rises to the top.

You have what it takes when it takes more than you
think you have. You are stronger than you know.

I have complete confidence, O God! I will sing and praise you! Wake up, my soul!

PSALM 108:1 GNT

Run Again

I run in the path of your commands,
for you have set my heart free.

PSALM 119:32 NIV

Walter Payton was one of the greatest running backs in the history of professional football. In his career, he gained more than nine miles in yardage. It is true that every 4.6 yards of the nine miles, someone knocked him down, but he always got up and ran again. He didn't let setbacks deter him from running toward the goal.

Every now and then, you get knocked down in your marriage, but you get up and run again. When dreams don't come true and plans don't work out, you keep dreaming and keep planning. When you think you were promised a rainbow but seem to get rain instead, you put your eyes to the sky and look through the clouds to the sun. You accept any splinters that might come to your marriage and look for that road of splendor you know is there.

You get up and run again. Adversity challenges you and brings out your best. You remember it takes both rain and sunlight to make a rainbow. An airplane takes off against the wind, not with it. What you are facing in your marriage becomes a source of ingenuity, creativity, and growth.

Opportunities in your marriage are disguised as difficulties.
The stream of adversity flows into the river of greatness.

*J*udgment will again be
founded on righteousness,
and all the upright in
heart will follow it.

PSALM 94:15 NIV

Side by Side

Your lovingkindness is before my eyes,
and I have walked in Your truth.

PSALM 26:3 NASB

In the Bedouin culture, a young man is not allowed to propose to a young woman or even approach her outright. Instead, he watches

her from afar as she tends her flock and, when night comes, goes to the place where she has watered her sheep at a well or a spring. He puts his footprint there in the sand so she will see it the next morning. When she goes to the watering spot the next day, she sees his footprint and, if she is interested in meeting him, places her footprint alongside his.

Your marriage is best when the two of you walk side by side. Side by side, courage increases and determination escalates. Walking together, you feel strength from the presence of the other. What is looked at with four eyes instead of two can be seen more clearly.

A team does better and goes farther. Individuals
play games. Teams win championships.

Teach me your way,
O Lord, that I may
walk in your truth; give
me an undivided heart
to revere your name.

Psalm 86:11 nrsv

Intertwined for Strength

Jerusalem, well-built city, built as a place for worship!
PSALM 122:3 THE MESSAGE

The huge redwood trees in California are the tallest trees in the world, some more than three hundred feet high and over twenty-five hundred years old. One would think they'd have root systems reaching down hundreds of feet into the ground and spread all over the place. Actually, they don't have deep root systems at all. Instead, the trees are intertwined. Locked together, the redwoods stand steady in the fiercest of storms.

The ideal of two people becoming one in marriage is better served when viewed not as amalgamation but as integration. Two people intertwined, wrapped up in each other, drawing strength from the individuality of each. Diversity that contributes but never loses sight of wholeness. That kind of unity is the birthplace of God's purpose for your marriage. In union, you are strong and true.

Keep together what God joins together.
Synchronize your lives in thought and deed.
Gather around a song and sing in harmony.

How wonderful it is,
how pleasant, for God's
people to live together
in harmony!

PSALM 133:1 GNT

I Affirm You

Our pride is in the name of the LORD our God.

PSALM 20:7 NRSV

Farley and Lana do an interesting thing before they call it a day. After they are in bed and have read a daily devotion, they brag on each other. Their exercise is ritualistic in nature and begins this way: "I was proud of you today when you _____." There follows some instance or instances when Farley was proud of Lana and she was proud of him. Often it's an accomplishment or achievement that is cited. Sometimes it's something one did for the other, or said to the other. Or something one said about the other to a friend or neighbor.

Affirmation is essential in your marriage. Let your mate know when he or she does something well. Don't keep the good stuff a secret. When the flower blossoms, compliment the gardener. Catch your mate doing something special and make a federal case out of it.

Your mate goes a long way on a compliment from you. Make your mate feel as important as he or she is.

My soul shall make its
boast in the LORD.

PSALM 34:2 NKJV

See the Best

O LORD, you protect me and save me; your care has made me
great, and your power has kept me safe.

PSALM 18:35 GNT

In the Bible, Gideon is a farmer who doesn't think much of himself. He is cowering in the face of an enemy and seriously depreciat-

ing himself. Then God sends an angel to
help Gideon with his self-esteem. The angel
addresses Gideon in an unexpected way. He
says to this man who doesn't think much of
himself, "The LORD is with you, mighty
warrior" (Judges 6:12 NIV). God doesn't
agree with Gideon's self-assessment, and
sends the angel to correct it.

See the best in your mate, and speak clearly about it. Say something about your mate's usefulness: "I couldn't have done that without you." Brag on skills and talents: "I don't know anybody who
can do that like you can." Notice family strengths: "You are so good
with our children." Compliment character: "You always tell the
truth." Let it be known you have noticed.

A sincere compliment is the least expensive and
most valuable gift you can give your mate.

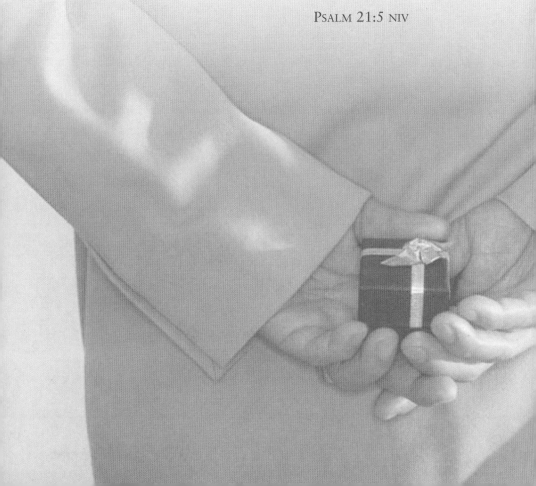

*Y*ou have bestowed
on him splendor
and majesty.

PSALM 21:5 NIV

Laugh and Last

He who sits in the heavens laughs.

PSALM 2:4 NASB

When you laugh together about yourselves as a couple, you create a bond of humanness. You say to one another that whatever happened is okay, and you are okay. Just because one or both faltered or fumbled doesn't mean the world's come to an end. It means an opportunity has come to affirm each other, get closer, and turn the page. Anoint whatever happened with laughter, and move on.

Mother Teresa required that the corridors and rooms of her healing homes be filled with laughter. She knew that laughter helps, holds, and heals. Fill your house with laughter. Let it ring with the sound of those who see what's funny about themselves. Laughter transforms tears into joy, the unbearable into the manageable, and a dead end into a freeway. Laughter is good for you and for your marriage.

Laughter is good exercise. It's like jogging on the inside. Make your mate laugh, and everything else falls into place.

Weeping may remain for
a night, but rejoicing
comes in the morning.

PSALM 30:5 NIV

Give Grace

You, LORD, are all I have, and you give me all I need.

PSALM 16:5 GNT

ob and Juanita came to an agreement not long after they were married that they would each make a list of things they would immediately forgive each other for when those particular things occurred. They called it their "grace" list. Neither saw their mate's list but, over the years, one would say to the other, "Forget about it, that's on the list." Forgiveness was given and received, and Bob or Juanita moved on with a clean slate.

Grace is what you don't necessarily deserve but get anyway, and your marriage does better where it is plentiful. When grace happens, resentment takes a hike and renewal blows its winds of enlightenment and empowerment upon your marriage. In the Bible, when the prodigal son returned home, his dad dashed down the road to extend to him the hand and heart of grace. All was forgiven.

Give grace to one another. Grace clears the road and builds bridges across the chasms. Grace makes crooked lines straight.

Clear my name, GOD;
I've kept an honest shop.
I've thrown in my lot
with you, GOD, and I'm
not budging.

PSALM 26:1 THE MESSAGE

Remember the Best

I can still hear them shout their joyful praises.

PSALM 42:4 CEV

A myth tells of a woman who wanted to cross the river to get to the region of departed spirits. She was required to drink water from the river. As she knelt to drink, a voice asked why she wanted to cross the river. She said so she could forget all she had suffered. "You will also forget what made you rejoice." The woman said she could forget her failures. "You will also forget your victories." The woman said she could forget how she'd been wronged. The voice responded, "You will also forget how you have been loved." The woman stood up and walked away from the river. She would retain the memory of the not-so-good for the sake of the memory of the best.

In your marriage, remember the good times, and they will be yours again. Nothing is lost that you remember well.

Good remembrances raise you up with their worth
and keep you there with their wonder.

I remembered my
songs in the night.

PSALM 77:6 NIV

Take Courage

Be strong and take heart, all you who hope in the LORD.

PSALM 31:24 NIV

Courage is good for your marriage. Without it, you stand still. With it, you move forward. Courage gives a push to your marriage if it is entrenched in sameness. It gives a pull to a relationship that has perhaps forgotten how to improve. Courage turns on the switch, the gears move, and your marriage picks up speed. Courage puts your marriage in the active voice. It gives you strength to do what you know to do, what you want to do.

With courage, you think more about what you can make happen than what is happening to you. You overcome fear through action. Instead of using the time to wish for something, you go after what you wish for. You believe it is what you do about what you know that counts. You don't wait for something to turn up. You go and turn something up.

A ship in the harbor is safe, but that is not what ships are built for. Your marriage was built to take action and move forward.

$\mathcal{H}$eaven belongs to the LORD alone, but he gave the earth to us humans.

PSALM 115:16 GNT

Give to Live

You, O LORD, are a merciful and gracious God.

PSALM 86:15 NLT

A fellow complained that his wife was always asking him for money. "Yesterday she asked me for a hundred dollars," he said to his friend. "The day before she wanted seventy five, and today she asked me for two hundred." His friend wanted to know what she did with all that money. The man replied, "I don't know. I never give her any."

Your marriage is better when you give to each other. Giving produces gratitude in the one who receives and immeasurable joy in the one who gives. When you give time to each other, that time stands still and wraps its bliss around your marriage. A well-chosen greeting card stuck in a mirror where it can't be missed is keenly understood. To enrich your marriage, you have a great variety of gifts from which to choose.

Your marriage lives by what you give to each other. When you love, you give. When you give, you love.

I will thank the LORD
because he is just; I will
sing praise to the name
of the LORD Most High.

PSALM 7:17 NLT

Flowers and So Forth

You enlarged my path under me, so my feet did not slip.

PSALM 18:36 NKJV

The young man was rather shy, and after she had thrown her arms around him and kissed him for bringing her a bouquet of flow-

ers, he jumped up and grabbed his hat. "Oh, don't go," she said as he made for the door. "I didn't mean to offend you."

He replied, "I'm not offended. I'm going for more flowers."

Little remembrances in your marriage have big power. They elicit appreciation and produce affection disproportionantly to their size or cost. A bouquet of flowers, a pair of socks to match a new shirt, a handwritten note, and a paperback book are some of many avenues open for you to express love to each other. A little goes a long way when it is thoughtful and sweet. It doesn't take much to say much. Sometimes, almost anything can come from almost nothing.

Be on the lookout for ways to say your love. Wrap your love creatively and imaginatively. Make it interesting.

Show me your unfailing
love in wonderful ways.

PSALM 17:7 NLT

It Comes Back

GOD makes his people strong. GOD gives his people peace.

PSALM 29:11 THE MESSAGE

Once there was a little boy who got angry with his mother. After she rebuked him, he ran off into the woods, stood on a hill, and yelled into the forest, "I hate you! I hate you!" Then he heard a voice coming back to him out of the forest, saying, "I hate you! I hate you!" He ran to his mother, crying, "There's a mean man in the woods yelling that he hates me."

His mother took him back to the hill and said, "Shout as loudly as you can into the woods, 'I love you! I love you!'"

The voice came back, "I love you! I love you!"

Your marriage is full of echoes. What goes around comes around. You get what you give. Sentiment, temperament, and attitude come back to you because they know the way.

In your marriage, there is a boomerang effect. Love imitates love. You stand in the shadow you cast.

I will praise the LORD at all times. I will constantly speak his praises.

PSALM 34:1 NLT

It Goes a Long Way

O taste and see that the LORD is good.

PSALM 34:8 NRSV

There is a lovely story about George Washington when he took command of the Continental Army at Cambridge, Massachusetts.

He found a ragged body of soldiers, some with only farm implements for weapons. A regiment from Connecticut looked particularly bad. Yet when that regiment was drawn up for Washington to inspect, he looked at them as if they were the finest in the world and said, "Gentlemen, I have great confidence in the men of Connecticut."

One of the soldiers later said, "I clasped my musket to my breast and said to myself, 'Let them come on.'"

In your marriage, a little encouragement goes a long way. Words of encouragement to each other fan the spark of potential into the flame of achievement. Encourage each other to high spots of resolve and confidence.

Encouragement is the least expensive and most valuable gift you can give each other. It is wind beneath your wings.

*T*hink of the wonderful
works he has done.

PSALM 105:5 NLT

Keep Talking

I will speak of your righteousness all day long.

PSALM 71:24 GNT

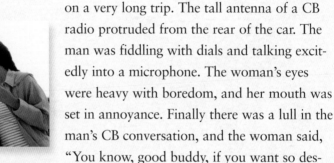

Years ago, a man and his wife were driving along a superhighway on a very long trip. The tall antenna of a CB radio protruded from the rear of the car. The man was fiddling with dials and talking excitedly into a microphone. The woman's eyes were heavy with boredom, and her mouth was set in annoyance. Finally there was a lull in the man's CB conversation, and the woman said, "You know, good buddy, if you want so desperately to communicate with somebody, you might try talking to me."

Talk clearly enough in your marriage to communicate, and there will be a meeting of persons and a sharing of life. Communicate intimately enough to commune, and you will experience a sacrament of relationship and love. Keep talking, and touch the eternal of each other.

Talk it over. Talk it out.
Talk it through. Talk it together.

They shall speak of the
glory of your kingdom.

PSALM 145:11 NRSV

Play Together

Sing praises to God and to his name!
Sing loud praises to him who rides the clouds.

PSALM 68:4 NLT

Pastor Ned sometimes got his words wrapped around his tongue and would say something he didn't intend to say. The words just didn't come out right. One Sunday, he had finished his sermon without verbal mishap and was giving the closing prayer. He ended the prayer by saying, "In Christ's name we play."

When you play together in your marriage, you stay together in your marriage. God blesses your play because play is heavenly. The Bible paints heaven as a place of celebration, joy, and fun. Heaven is much more about play than it is about work. It may even be one long vacation. If you have a lot of downtime in your marriage, you will have a lot of uptime in the quality of your relationship. Take fun-filled holidays together, and your holidays will become holy days of praise and thanksgiving.

Get serious about not being serious. Play and
laugh together. Let loose and surrender to the joy
God puts in your hearts.

Ascribe to the LORD,
O sons of the mighty,
ascribe to the LORD
glory and strength.

PSALM 29:1 NASB

Keep the Fire Burning

Hailstones and fiery coals lit up the sky in front of you.
Psalm 18:12 CEV

A man came out of a house and went next door with an empty shovel in his hand. A few minutes later, he emerged and went back to his own house, but his shovel was no longer empty. It was full of hot, burning coals that he balanced evenly and carried carefully. He made his way through the door to his house and up the stairs to a fireplace where he placed the burning coals on top of smoldering ashes. Soon the fireplace was full of flame.

Keep the fire of your marriage burning. Let the flame of love burn hot on the hearth of your commitment to each other. Blow on your marriage the breath of encouragement and support. Pour the oil of faith and fervor on it and set it ablaze with warmth and passion.

Keep in touch with the fire of God's love and hope for you. That fire always warms, always burns.

The voice of the LORD
divides the flames of fire.

PSALM 29:7 NKJV

Invite Change

*We won't be afraid! Let the earth tremble and the
mountains tumble into the deepest sea.*

PSALM 46:2 CEV

*I*n the movie *Lawrence of Arabia*, Lawrence risks his life to rescue a colleague by crossing the hottest part of the desert in the middle of the day. His friends tell him he's crazy to go back into the desert because "it is written" that nobody can survive the heat. Lawrence succeeds in his rescue and, upon his return, triumphantly declares to his friends, "Nothing is written."

Nothing is written in your marriage that says you cannot do what you have not done, go where you have not been, or be who you have not become. Change is good. It gets you from one location to another and helps you stand in a new place. It enables you to paint a new picture, sing a new song, and surround yourself with fresh opportunities and possibilities. Change is good for you and for your marriage.

*It is never too late or too early to change. Lift your
sails to new winds, and go to new places.*

*S*ing to him a new song.

PSALM 33:3 NIV

Want the Ball

I run the way of your commandments,
for you enlarge my understanding.

PSALM 119:32 NRSV

wo teams played a football game, and one dominated the other. The outclassed team's only hope was to give the ball to Jenkins, the fastest player on either team. The coach told his quarterback to give the ball to Jenkins on the first play, but he didn't. The coach signaled for the quarterback to give Jenkins the ball on the second play, but the running back did not get the ball. Same for the third and fourth plays. As the offensive team came off the field, the coach screamed at the quarterback, "I told you four times to give the ball to Jenkins."

The quarterback replied, "But Jenkins doesn't want the ball."

You want the ball in your marriage. You take responsibility, and you are responsible. You don't duck what comes to you. You don't defer to another. You start, continue, finish, and follow through.

You take responsibility in your marriage.
You don't ask another to do what you can do.

O my people, listen to my teaching.
Open your ears to what I am saying.

PSALM 78:1 NLT

Meet Problems Together

He opened up a rock, and water gushed out to form
a river through the dry and barren land.

PSALM 105:41 NLT

Problems in your marriage are a good sign. They mean your marriage is going somewhere. The road may be bumpy, but you are moving forward on it. You can avoid the bumps by sitting still, but you don't intend to do that. You like the road, and you want to be on it. Problems come along, but the journey is good.

Problems are stones against the knife of commitment that sharpen the abilities, talents, and skills of both of you. When you meet your problems together, you can do something about them. You challenge your problems because you know they are a glorious invitation to discover how effective you are together. A problem is a chance for the two of you to do your best as partners in marriage. Problems are God's gift to help you change and grow, extend, and expand as one.

Nothing is hard if each of you takes a portion of it. The
best way out of a difficulty is to go through it together.

Even though I walk
through the valley of
the shadow of death,
I fear no evil.

PSALM 23:4 NASB

Show It

O Lord, open my lips, and my mouth will declare your praise.

PSALM 51:15 NRSV

Marriages are built on small expressions of affection. It doesn't take much to say a lot. Affection shown is readily known. Hold the hand of your mate, and time stands still. Wink at your mate across a room, and oceans roar. Touch a shoulder as you pass by, and symphonies play. Put firm hands on a back, massage it, and heaven descends. There are many ways to express affection.

But also remember to say it. Say "I love you" at every opportunity. There are no three better words. It may go without saying, but don't let it go unsaid. And don't forget "honey," "darling," and "sweetheart." These are words easily understood and greatly appreciated. Be a liaison between your feelings and your words. Get them from your heart into your head and onto your lips.

Love knows no muteness. It has no muzzles.
Love says what it thinks.

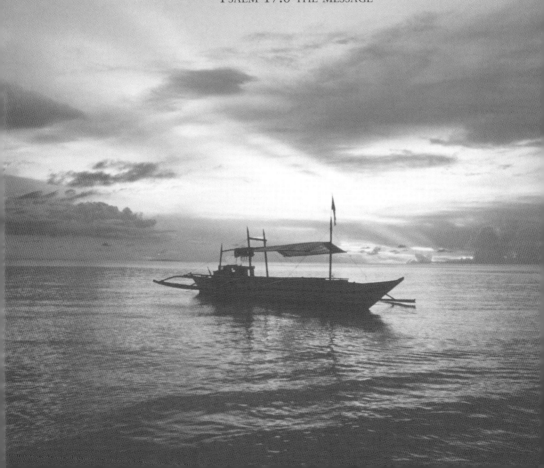

I call to you, GOD, because
I'm sure of an answer. So—
answer! bend your ear!
listen sharp!

PSALM 17:6 THE MESSAGE

Lift Your Faith

O my God, I trust in You.

PSALM 25:2 NKJV

Only God can meet the needs of your marriage. Go it alone, and it won't go. Partner in faith with God, and reap great blessings.

Your marriage is God's idea and, because of that, needs God's presence. Your marriage is God shaped and, without God, gets out of shape. But, with God in your marriage on a daily basis, it has form, substance, and power. Deep faith, like a strongly rooted tree, stands firm when storms come. And your marriage stands with it.

God has many doors through which, in your marriage, you enter into depth and richness. Knock on those doors with the hands of faith. God has many heights to which you will ascend and many summits on which you will stand. Climb those heights with steps of faith and stand on those summits in the glorious assurance that God is with you.

You do not possess faith so much as faith possesses you. You yearn, dream, and walk by faith.

As for me, I trust in You,
O LORD; I say, "You are
my God."

PSALM 31:14 NKJV

Surrender All

I will fulfill my vows to you, O God, and offer
a sacrifice of thanks for your help.

PSALM 56:12 NLT

Give your marriage to God each day. Give him all of it. When you give all of your marriage each day to God, an undertow of divine presence sweeps you into the depths of significance and meaning. Put yourselves and your marriage in the hands and heart of God. Surrender is the key.

It is letting go that makes you strong in your marriage. Give up control to God. Say yes to God in all facets and phases of your marriage. Don't hold anything back. Surrender makes you shapable and teachable. It gets you empty enough to be filled. God can do wonders with your marriage when you give him all parts of it. How well you do in your marriage depends on whose hands you put it in.

When you give your marriage to God, he comes to you
and works through you. His presence is your power.

Trust the LORD and his
mighty power.

PSALM 105:4 CEV

Notes